Searchlight
BOOKS™

What
Can We
Learn from Early
Civilizations?

Tools and Treasures of

Ancient China

Candice Ransom

Lerner Publications Company
Minneapolis

To my editor, Laura

Lerner Publications Company
A division of Lerner Publishing Group, Inc.
241 First Avenue North
Minneapolis, MN 55401 U.S.A.

For reading levels and more information, look up this title at www.lernerbooks.com.

Library of Congress Cataloging-in-Publication Data

Ransom, Candice F., 1952–
    Tools and treasures of ancient China / Candice Ransom.
        pages ˙ cm. — (Searchlight books™. What can we learn from early civilizations?)
    Includes index.
    ISBN 978–1–4677–1428–0 (library binding)
    ISBN 978–1–4677–2504–0 (eBook)
    1. China—Civilization—Juvenile literature. I. Title.
    DS721.R26 2014
    931—dc23   2013022271

Manufactured in the United States of America
1 – PC – 12/31/13

Contents

Chapter 1

THE ANCIENT CHINESE

Ancient China got its start more than four thousand years ago. It is one of the world's oldest civilizations.

Some of the world's greatest inventors came from China. What else did the ancient Chinese do?

The ancient Chinese had great artists, builders, and thinkers. They had doctors, scientists, and mapmakers. They made important discoveries. And they invented things we still use. These inventions are just some of the treasures the ancient Chinese left behind.

This gate marks the entrance to the ancient city of Anyang. The city is still a part of modern China.

Two Rivers

Ancient China was in East Asia. Ancient China lay in the eastern part of modern China. It was isolated from other peoples and lands. Seas lay to the east. The steep Himalayan mountains rose up in the south and the west. The Gobi Desert lay far to the north. These barriers made it hard to enter or leave China.

Mount Everest (FAR RIGHT) **is the world's tallest mountain. It is in the Himalayas.**

▼

Two rivers divided ancient China. The early Chinese farmed along the Yellow River. The river carries rich soil. The soil is good for growing grains and other crops. The Yangtze River was an important source of food. Fishing boats sailed its deep waters.

Dynasties

Powerful families called dynasties ruled China for
thousands of years. The same family stayed in power
for generations. The Xia dynasty came first. It ruled
China until about 1600 BCE. Very little is known about it.

This ancient cup was discovered in the Henan Province of China. The Xia dynasty ruled over this land.

The Shang
dynasty ruled for
the next 550 years.
The Zhou dynasty
ruled for another
800 years. These
families helped
make China a
great civilization.

**This painting shows the
first ruler of the Shang
dynasty, King Tang.**

Ancient China was made up of many states. Each state had its own leaders. Some states were large. Others were the size of a town.

People have uncovered the remains of ancient Chinese villages in modern times. This one is from the Zhou dynasty.

Ancient China

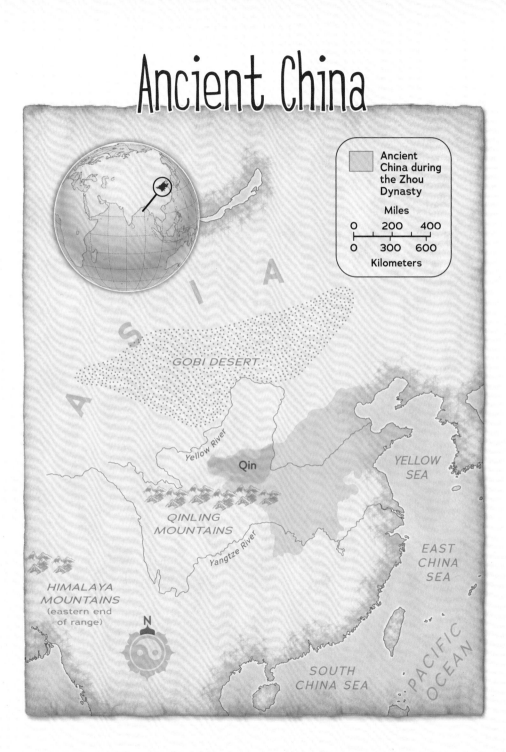

Chapter 2

DAILY LIFE

Everyone in ancient China had a role. People were split into groups by their jobs. The largest group was the peasants. Peasants had very little power.

This painting shows peasants harvesting rice. What other crops did farmers grow in ancient China?

Peasants farmed the land but did not own it. Chinese farmers grew a grain called millet. They also grew rice, barley, peas, beans, wheat, and hemp.

Both people and animals can eat millet. That made it a very useful grain to the ancient Chinese.

These famous ancient clay statues show a powerful Chinese army. They were created after the end of the Zhou dynasty.

Along with the peasants were other groups. Craftspeople made pottery, chariots, and weapons. Merchants sold goods at the markets. Soldiers defended the country from outsiders. Sometimes soldiers also fought in wars among the Chinese states.

Rich landowners formed the highest and smallest group. They were known as the nobles. Nobles held a leadership role. They ran the states, cities, and villages. Some were in charge of the markets. Others set prices for goods. Nobles also led soldiers in war. They drove into battle on chariots pulled by horses.

This old Chinese bronze artwork shows a noble riding a chariot. The chariot was a sign of power and leadership.

Communication

Ancient Chinese people spoke an old form of the Chinese language. Both the ancient and modern Chinese use characters instead of letters. Characters are small pictures. Each picture stands for a word. The character for *to shoot* is a picture of an arrow across a bow. The character for *west* is a picture of a bird in a nest.

The writing on this bone, from the Shang dynasty, is more than three thousand years old.

The Chinese wrote on strips of bamboo and silk scrolls. They used a brush dipped in ink. The writing was read from top to bottom.

The ancient Chinese used writing tools such as these.

Religion

The ancient Chinese believed in many gods. There were gods of the sun, moon, and wind. There were water, soil, and other gods too.

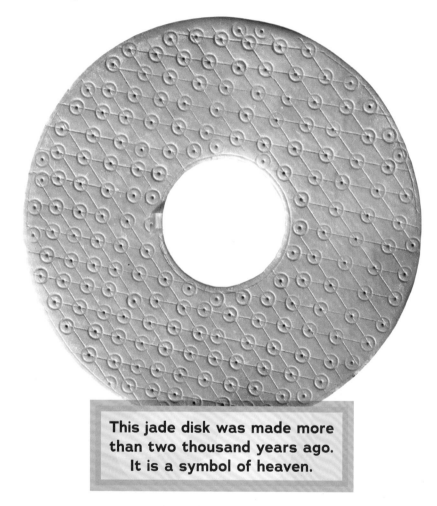

This jade disk was made more than two thousand years ago. It is a symbol of heaven.

The people believed that the gods controlled the seasons. The seasons were important to farming and hunting. But only nobles were allowed to practice the Chinese religion. They did it for the good of all the people.

CHINESE NOBLES PERFORMED
IMPORTANT RELIGIOUS CEREMONIES.

Some Chinese nobles were also fortune-tellers. They used "dragon bones" to ask the gods about the future. The bones weren't really from dragons. They were turtle shells and shoulder blades from cattle.

These oracle bones came from the Shang dynasty. The one on the left is a tortoise shell.

First, a nobleman would ask one of the gods a question. He might ask, "Will it rain soon?" Next, holes were drilled in a dragon bone. Then it was heated until it cracked. The nobleman studied the cracks. The pattern of the cracks had a special meaning. It told him the god's answer.

The nobles in this carving are offering gifts to the gods for good fortune.

Chapter 3

THE CULTURE OF ANCIENT CHINA

Ancient China had an advanced culture. The ancient Chinese discovered how to make silk from silkworms. They created a calendar based on the movement of the moon. They invented strong boats. And they invented the bow and arrow.

Chinese silk workers boil silkworm cocoons in this painting. What else did the ancient Chinese make?

Artwork

Early Chinese people made beautiful clay vases and pots. The pottery was painted with swirls and other designs.

Artists during the Shang dynasty invented a way to shape bronze metal. They melted the metal. Then they poured it into clay molds. The molds were shaped like cups, animal figures, and swords. The liquid bronze cooled and hardened. Then the clay mold was taken away.

A metalworker from the Shang dynasty made this bronze figure.

Ancient China is also known for its jade carvings. This hard stone was very valuable. It represented eternal life. Noblewomen in the Zhou dynasty wore jade necklaces. Noblemen carried fancy jade knives. Some nobles were even buried in a suit carved from jade!

CAN YOU IMAGINE HOW HEAVY A SUIT MADE OF JADE STONES WOULD BE?

Architecture

Most buildings in China were made from earth. Peasants lived in huts. These small houses were made of dried mud. The mud was shaped into hard bricks. The roofs were made of woven straw.

Modern Chinese farmers still make houses from mud with straw roofs. This photo was taken in 1945.

This clay model is of a Chinese noble's palace. It was buried with the noble more than two thousand years ago.

Noble families lived in large houses. The richest of them lived in palaces. To build a palace, workers first built a wooden frame. Next, they pounded dirt inside the frame. They took the frame down. Then they scraped the walls smooth. A higher wall surrounded the palace.

Nobles were buried in fancy structures too. These underground graves were called tombs. Inside a tomb was a noble's most valued treasures. The bodies of nobles have been found with bronze cups and jade axes. Sometimes their servants and animals were even buried with them!

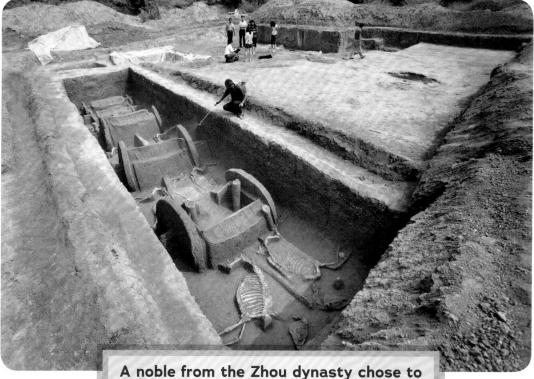

A noble from the Zhou dynasty chose to be buried with his horses and chariots.

Pastimes

Each village had its own market. This was the center of the community. On market day, the nobleman in charge of the market raised his flag. This marked a joyful time for the villagers. They flocked to the merchants' stalls. They bought food, pottery, and cloth.

The Chinese people in this ancient brick carving are buying and selling goods at a market.

Girls and boys also met to exchange flowers. And grown-ups chatted with friends and neighbors. That was how they learned what was happening in their village.

Children played together during market days, while grown-ups went shopping.

Everyone enjoyed the Chinese festivals. These events took place throughout the year. The most important one was the spring festival. It celebrated the end of winter. People gathered at the rivers to tell jokes and talk. Drums thumped, and children danced. This festival came to be known as the Chinese New Year.

This brick carving shows people dancing and talking at an ancient Chinese festival.

Pangu Separates Sky and Earth

The ancient Chinese passed down many stories. One was of Pangu. His tale tells how the ancient Chinese thought heaven and earth were created.

In the beginning, the whole universe fit inside a huge black egg. A man named Pangu hatched from the egg. The top half of the shell was the sky. The bottom half was the earth.

Pangu grew taller every day for eighteen thousand years. As he grew, he pushed the top and bottom halves of the egg apart. He also created many things. He separated hot from cold, light from dark, and male from female. Finally, Pangu stopped growing. The sky became heaven. And Earth became the world we know.

Chapter 4

IMPERIAL CHINA

The last five hundred years of ancient China were a time of war. The Chinese states fought one another to control the land. In 221 BCE, an army from the state of Qin attacked the Zhou dynasty. Warriors rode on horseback. They defeated Zhou soldiers in their clumsy chariots.

Emperor Qin was the first to rule Imperial China. What is Imperial China famous for?

The Qin dynasty took over China. The dynasty united the country under one government. The age of ancient China ended. And Imperial China began. Imperial China is known for many great inventions. Gunpowder, paper, compasses, and kites are just a few.

This artwork shows two Chinese scientists inventing the compass.

The Qin dynasty wanted to protect China from its enemies. Its workers began building the Great Wall of China. The wall was made from pounded earth and stone. The Great Wall is the world's longest human-made structure. It stretches for 4,000 miles (6,400 kilometers)!

Tourists often walk along this part of the Great Wall of China. It is just outside the city of Beijing.

Imperial China is also known for the Silk Road. The Chinese traded with other countries on this route. They exchanged Chinese silk for gold, glass, and other goods. The Silk Road went from China to Pakistan, India, and Rome. People traveled it by camel and on foot.

People still travel on camels through the deserts that were part of the Silk Road.

China Today

The rule of dynasties ended in 1912. China's modern government came to power in 1949. China became known as the People's Republic of China. More than 1.3 billion people live in modern China. No other country has as many people.

Schoolchildren wave Chinese flags.

MANY MODERN CHINESE CITIES
HAVE BECOME BOOMING CENTERS
FOR WORLDWIDE BUSINESS.

▼

Ancient China is long gone. But it has not been forgotten. The ancient Chinese left behind their pottery, writings, and dragon bones. These are reminders of China's long and amazing history.

Glossary

bamboo: tall woody grass with hollow stems

bronze: metal made of copper and tin

character: a mark or a symbol used in writing

chariot: a two-wheeled horse-drawn cart used in battle

civilization: a large society in which people share a common government and culture

dynasty: a ruling family that rules for many years

hemp: a plant grown for its fibers that are used to make rope

jade: a hard green gemstone

merchant: a buyer and seller of goods

millet: a type of grain

noble: a person of high birth or rank

peasant: a farmer of low social rank

tomb: a burial place for the dead

Learn More about Ancient China

Books

Friedman, Mel. *Ancient China*. New York: Children's Press, 2010. Read about clay soldiers, Yu the Great, and the Forbidden City.

Kramer, Lance. *Great Ancient China Projects You Can Build Yourself.* White River Junction, VT: Nomad Press, 2008. Learn about Chinese inventions with fun, hands-on activities.

Ping, Wang. *The Dragon Emperor.* Minneapolis: Millbrook Press, 2008. Read this ancient Chinese tale about a very special emperor and the challenges he faces when the evil Chi You tries to overthrow him.

Riehecky, Janet. *China*. Minneapolis: Lerner Publications, 2008. Read about modern Chinese geography, customs, holidays, families, and more in this lively book.

Websites

Ancient China for Kids
http://www.china.mrdonn.org
Visit this website for history, games, clip art, and crafts about ancient China.

Ancient China: Inventions and Technology
http://ducksters.com/history/china/inventions_technology.php
Learn how the early Chinese invented gunpowder, the compass, and woodblock printing.

Enchanted Learning: All about China
http://www.enchantedlearning.com/asia/china
Find fun facts about modern China.

LERNER
SOURCE

Expand learning beyond the printed book. Download free, complementary educational resources for this book from our website, www.lerneresource.com.

Index

Photo Acknowledgments

The images in this book are used with the permission of: © Hungchungchih/Dreamstime.com, pp. 4, 15; © Keren Su/China Span/Getty Images, p. 5; © Blasbike/Dreamstime.com, p. 6; © Bepi Ghoitti /Studio Box/Photographers Choice RF/Getty Images, p. 7; © TAO Images Limited/Getty Images, p. 8; PD-Art/Wikimedia Commons, p. 9; © Luo Xiaoguang/Xinhua Press/CORBIS, p. 10; © Laura Westlund/Independent Picture Service, p. 11; The Granger Collection, New York, pp. 12, 20 (left), 22; © iStockphoto.com/fotohunter, p. 13; © iStockphoto.com/gautier075, p. 14; © Lowell Georgia /CORBIS, p. 16; © Fotosearch/SuperStock, p. 17; © G. Dagli Orti/De Agostini Picture Library/Getty Images, pp. 18, 23; © Private Collection/De Agostini Picture Library/The Bridgeman Art Library, p. 19; © Art Resource, NY, p. 20 (right); Image copyright © The Metropolitan Museum of Art. Image source: Art Resource, NY, p. 21; © E. Lessing/De Agostini Picture Library/Getty Images, p. 24; © NGS Image Collection/The Art Archive at Art Resource, NY, p. 25; Gary L. Todd, Ph.D., Professor of History, Sias International University, Xinzheng, China, pp. 26, 28, 30; © Zhang Xiaoli/CORBIS, p. 27; © Bibliotheque des Arts Decoratifs, Paris, France/Archives Charmet/The Bridgeman Art Library, p. 29; © iStockphoto.com/Hanquan Chen, p. 31; © The Art Archive/SuperStock, p. 32; © AISA/Everett Collection, p. 33; © bjdlzx/Getty Images, p. 34; © Rocguan1210/Dreamstime.com, p. 35; © Jlhope/ Dreamstime.com, p. 36; © Tomohiro Ohsumi/Bloomberg/Getty Images, p. 37.

Front cover: © iStockphoto.com/Hanquan Chen.

Main body text set in Adrianna Regular 14/20
Typeface provided by Chank